Learning About Atoms

By
SUSAN KNORR

COPYRIGHT © 2004 Mark Twain Media, Inc.

ISBN 1-58037-271-6

Printing No. CD-1631

Mark Twain Media, Inc., Publishers
Distributed by Carson-Dellosa Publishing Company, Inc.

The purchase of this book entitles the buyer to reproduce the student pages for classroom use only. Other permissions may be obtained by writing Mark Twain Media, Inc., Publishers.

All rights reserved. Printed in the United States of America.

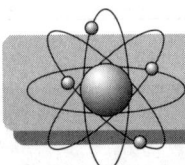

Table of Contents

Introduction: What Is an Atom? 1

The History of the Atom 2

Matter and the Atom 4

The Basics of the Atom 6
    The Parts of the Atom 6
    Creating a Three-Dimensional Model of the Atom 9
    Everything Is Made of Atoms! 11

The Periodic Table 13
    Atoms and the Periodic Table 13
    Groups and Periods 17
    Element PowerPoint® Presentation 20
        MLA and APA Source Cards 22

Isotopes 24
    Everything You Wanted to Know About Isotopes! 24
    Carbon Dating 28
    The Isotopes of Pennies: Activity and Investigation 30
    Uses of Carbon Dating 32
    Radioactive Decay of the Penny: Activity and Investigation 34

Research a Famous Scientist and Share His/Her Discovery 36
    Famous Scientist Report 36
    Research a Famous Scientist 37

Atoms Vocabulary 38
Atoms Crossword Puzzle 39
Jeopardy! Review Game 40
Atoms Unit Test 42
References Page 44
Answer Keys 45

Introduction: What Is an Atom?

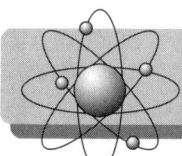

Everything in our world is made up of atoms, and this explains why atoms are called the building blocks of matter. These building blocks make up the air you breathe, the desk at which you are sitting, the paper and ink used in this book, and your body, which reacts to all of these things.

There are 94 (latest count) naturally occurring kinds of atoms. Naturally occurring atoms are those found in nature. We are also able to create about 25 more in the science laboratory. Every atom has the same parts, and the most notable of these are the **proton**, **neutron**, and **electron**. It took many years before these basic parts were identified. As with most scientific discoveries, some very bright people thought and thought about the origin of things and came up with the idea of the atom. Of course, many other people thought the idea of the atom was absurd—how could all things be made of something so small that it can't be seen? Remember that Democritus was the first person to develop the atomic theory, and he was a Greek philosopher living around 460 B.C.! Since then, many new discoveries have been made and will continue to be developed as new equipment allows us to "see" more clearly the amazing atom.

In this book, you will be able to trace the development of the theory of the atom and the resulting understandings, such as atomic structure and the periodic table. Each lesson provides the necessary background to move to the next level of both skill and conceptual development. While working your way through the lessons, you will have an opportunity to create an Element PowerPoint® Presentation. In-depth research of a specific element helps to develop technology and communication skills with the added bonus of creating "experts" with a passion for learning more.

The next area of focus forces you, the student, to deal head-on with the concept of isotopes and their role in our life right now! And last but not least, you will also be able to use your excitement and communication skills to role-play the life and scientific milestones of a scientist who contributed to our current understanding of the atom. So, student observers, put on those thinking caps and use your process skills to observe, classify, analyze, debate, design, and report. This unit contains a variety of lessons that will help you practice scientific processes as you make exciting discoveries about our ever-evolving understanding of the atom and how it affects our lives on Planet Earth!

The History of the Atom

As with most scientific discoveries, some very bright people thought and thought about the origin of things and came up with the idea of the atom. Of course, many other people thought the idea of the atom was absurd—how could all things be made of something so small that it can't be seen? Remember that Democritus was the first person to develop atomic theory, and he was a Greek philosopher living around 460 B.C.!

It took many years for the idea of atoms to catch on. In fact, it became increasingly important to try to prove that atoms did exist. In the late 1700s, John Dalton developed the **atomic theory** on which all current understandings are based. And where, you might wonder, did he come up with his ideas? Well, Dalton started out his career as a teacher of mathematics and natural philosophy. His constant search to better understand the subjects he taught caused him to conduct experiments to test his questions or hypotheses. Dalton set a fine example for scientists to follow because he recorded all of his work in journals, and he posted a whopping 200,000 entries! Most notable of the entries were those of his meteorological observations, which recorded the changeable climate of the Lake District where he lived in England.

John Dalton

The next few discoveries came in just a few years by three scientists. In the 1890s, J.J. Thomson discovered the **electron**. Many of his experiments with the cathode ray led him to believe in the existence of an atomic particle "with a mass about 1,000 times smaller than a hydrogen atom." As Thomson lectured to many scholars in England and America, his ideas met with much skepticism. The lack of the support of his colleagues caused him to work even harder to prove what he knew existed … the electron.

The "Plum Pudding" model of the atom proposed by J.J. Thomson

In 1919, Ernest Rutherford discovered the **proton**, and as he continued testing ideas, he developed the idea of the **nucleus** of the atom. He also proposed the idea of another particle (the neutron), which would be located in the nucleus with the proton. Many of Rutherford's ideas about atomic theory resulted from the experiments he conducted involving radiation. He was certain that both positive and negative charges were emitted by the atom. Since Thomson had identified the existence of the negatively charged electron, Rutherford proposed the idea of a positively charged proton. With further studies, he found that each of these particles was found in a specific location relative to one another and drew models to represent his ideas.

Ernest Rutherford and the Nuclear Atom model

The History of the Atom (cont.)

Rutherford was credited with introducing the terms: *alpha, beta,* and *gamma rays, the proton, half-life,* and *daughter atoms.*

James Chadwick, a student of Rutherford, is credited with the discovery of the **neutron**. Chadwick's discovery resulted from learning from others and using this knowledge to further his own ideas. He was able to study under Rutherford but was intrigued when the scientists Frederic and Irene Joliot-Curie proposed a different method for tracking particle radiation. Chadwick was able to use the work of Rutherford, Curie, and Joliot to successfully determine that the neutron did exist and that its mass was about 0.1 percent more than the proton's.

Niels Bohr proposed the Electron Shell model of the atom.

Many other scientists seized these ideas. During the process of discussing and explaining their thoughts, many developed models to help others understand the concept. The first model to gain acceptance was one proposed by Niels Bohr in the 1920s, which gave the particles of the atom a specific structure in which to reside. Bohr was a student of J.J. Thomson and won the Nobel Prize in physics in 1922 for his model. He was only 37 years old at the time of the award!

Now that scientists accepted the existence of the atom, they were beginning to realize that there were many different atoms. These atoms had both similar and unique characteristics. In 1869, Dmitri Mendeleev, a Russian chemist, arranged the 63 known elements into groups and periods and called it the **Periodic Table of the Elements**. His understanding of chemical properties and atomic weights allowed him to leave spaces open for yet-to-be-discovered elements.

In 1939, Niels Bohr informed the United States of the latest development of Nazi Germany, the splitting of the atom. The United States realized that the Nazis could develop extremely powerful weapons. As a result, President Franklin Roosevelt established the Manhattan Project in 1941. Robert Oppenheimer was appointed to head the project, which he established at Los Alamos, New Mexico. He was able to assemble the best minds in physics to develop the atomic bomb. The development of the atomic bomb is credited also to the preceding discoveries of scientists. Most notable among these scientists were James Chadwick, Enrico Fermi, Otto Hahn, Fritz Strassmann, and Lise Meitner. The Los Alamos Research Facility is still in existence and is known to be one of the finest in the world.

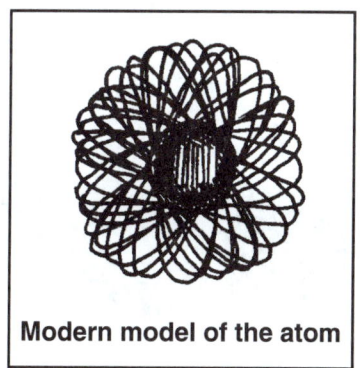

Modern model of the atom

Many new discoveries will become a reality as new equipment allows us to "see" more clearly the amazing atom.

Matter and the Atom

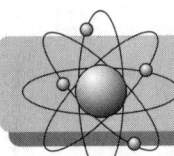

The atom is the smallest part of anything, and the universe is collectively the largest, yet both are closely related. Everything is made of matter, and all matter is made of atoms; this idea can present an interesting way of looking at everything in the universe.

So … what is an atom? Well … everything in our world is made of atoms, and this explains why atoms are called the building blocks of matter. These building blocks make up the air you breathe, the desk at which you are sitting, the paper and ink used in this book, and your body, which reacts to all of these things.

There are 94 (the latest count) naturally occurring kinds of atoms. **Naturally occurring** atoms are those not made in the laboratory. We are also able to create about 25 more atoms, which are referred to as **synthetic atoms**. All of this is well and good, but what does the atom look like? Again, this is an interesting question. Scientists are only able to give you their best guess, which has been changed many times and will continue to change as technology becomes increasingly more sophisticated.

To explain atoms, it is probably easier to start with the larger picture and work our way to the smallest. **Matter** is the term we use to explain anything that has mass and takes up space. If we were to look at air, we would find that 99.9% of the air is made of the elements nitrogen, oxygen, and argon. When we say that air is matter, we are referring to all of the elements. We can further break each of the three elements down to the billions and billions of atoms that make up the elements.

If you found this explanation somewhat helpful, let's try another example to cement the concept. An **atom** is the simplest form of matter that cannot be changed into a simpler form by ordinary means. An **element** is many of the same kind of atom. An example of this is when you have a piece of aluminum foil. This would be the element aluminum because it is many of the same kind of atom. If you tear a piece of aluminum from the roll and then keep tearing it into smaller and smaller pieces, you will eventually have a pile of aluminum specks that are good for nothing, but one could say that it is a pile of aluminum. The aluminum speck, while hardly visible to the human eye, contains millions and millions of aluminum atoms, each having the exact same properties of aluminum. Some of these properties include shiny, metal, solid at room temperature, and flexible as a thin sheet of aluminum. An atom, therefore, is the smallest part that anything can be broken down into and that still retains the properties of the element.

Diamond   **Graphite**   **Gold**   **Sulfur**   **Silver**
(both forms of carbon)

The Parts of the Atom (cont.)

There are some problems in showing the atom as a two-dimensional model. The size of the particles (protons, neutrons, and electrons) is not accurate because we know the electrons are 1,800 times smaller than the protons and neutrons. Also, the space between the nucleus and the first energy level of the electron cloud is much too close. While the protons and neutrons remain relatively stationary, the electrons spin very fast. The "circles" are meant to show that the electrons have an orbit pattern, but the pattern lines do not exist. I like to think of electrons as the blades on a fan. When the fan is turned off, we can see the individual blades (electrons). However, when the fan is on and the blades are spinning around the center point, we can only see a path pattern where the blades (electrons) are spinning. The only way to see the individual blades when they are spinning is to blink very quickly.

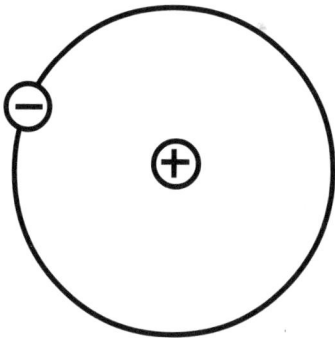

Hydrogen

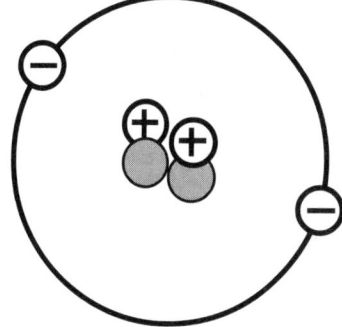

Helium

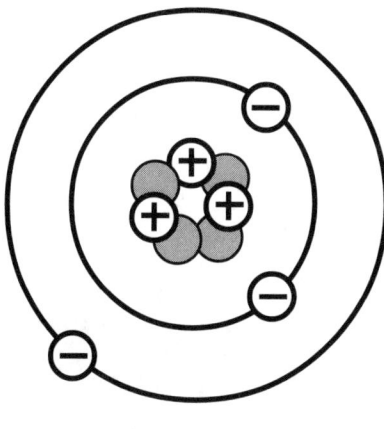

Lithium

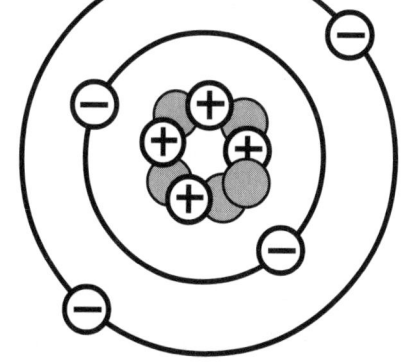

Beryllium

Learning About Atoms

The Parts of the Atom: Reinforcement Activity

Name: _____ Date: _____

To the student observer: What are the parts of the atom? _____
_____

Analyze: Why do scientists use models of the atom when we know that they are not completely accurate?
_____
_____

Directions: Answer the following questions about the atom.

1. The atom can be divided into _____ basic parts.
2. The three particles of the atom are the _____, _____, and _____.
3. The protons and neutrons are located in the _____.
4. The electrons are found in the _____.
5. The electrons spin around or _____ the nucleus.
6. The nucleus contains which atomic particles? _____ and _____.
7. The electron cloud contains which atomic particles? _____

What are the charges of the particles?

8. protons _____   9. neutrons _____   10. electrons _____

Look at the two-dimensional model of the atom. How many of each of the following do you find?

11. protons _____
12. neutrons _____
13. electrons _____
14. What is the weight of the nucleus of this atom? _____
15. An atom is very, very small. If you were to look at one atom through a microscope, what would take up most of the viewing area? _____
_____

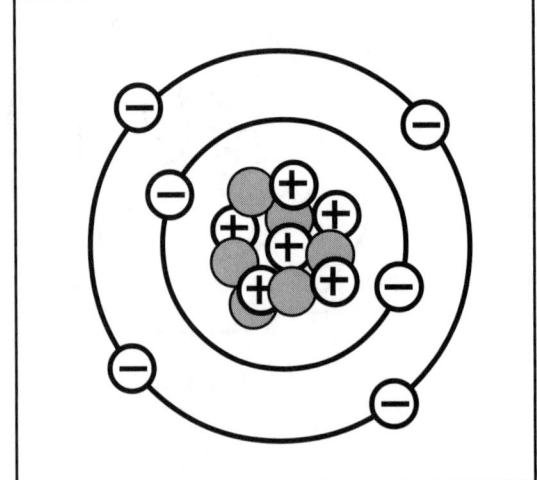

© Mark Twain Media, Inc., Publishers

Creating a Three-Dimensional Model of the Atom

Choose an atom with 20 protons or less. But where do you go to look for the number of protons? Well ... let's get a sneak preview of the Periodic Table of the Elements. There is usually a sample element box to explain how to gather information about a certain element (many of the same atom). Here is an example:

Atomic Number | 6   2 | **Electron Distribution**
  | 4 |
  | **C**   Carbon |
  | Atomic Mass 12 |

And now you may want a little help in understanding some of the new terms like **atomic number**. This number represents the number of protons in the carbon atom. The electron distribution tells how many electrons are found in each energy level. (Did you notice that the number of protons and electrons is exactly the same?) However, it doesn't tell us the number of neutrons, and those are the three particles we need to show on our 3-D model. The trick here is to look at the mass number. This represents the total number of protons and neutrons found in the nucleus. So to find the neutrons, simply do the math:

atomic mass (protons + neutrons) - atomic number (protons) = number of neutrons

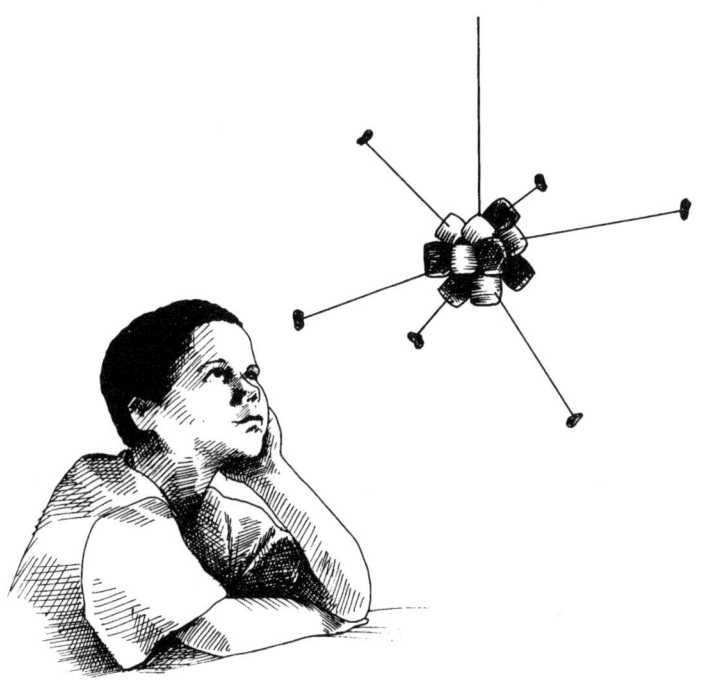

Now that you know how to find an atom with 20 protons or less, pick the atom that you will use to make a 3-D model. But what exactly will the project look like when it is completed? It might end up looking like a mobile that we used to make in grade school with clothes hanger circles representing energy levels and the nucleus dangling in the center. It may end up being a poster board with marshmallows piled up in the center representing the protons and neutrons (different colors, of course) and raisins stuck on the ends of toothpicks that extend outward from the nucleus. The first two toothpicks representing the first energy level will be the shortest, with the second energy level longer, the third energy level even longer, and so on.

Learning About Atoms

Creating a Three-Dimensional Model of the Atom

Name _____ Date: _____

Creating a Three-Dimensional Model of the Atom (cont.)

Do a little thinking and planning. Ask some people what they are doing and go from there. Remember the famous scientist we already learned about and how he built upon the ideas of other scientists? By following the example of these scientists, you can create a model that demonstrates your understanding of the concept and your unique creativity. Have fun!

Here is the grading rubric for the model project; take a look.

Components	2 points	1 point	0 points
Protons	Number is correct	—	Incorrect number
Neutrons	Number is correct	—	Incorrect number
Electrons	Number is correct	—	Incorrect number
Nucleus	• Correct particle found here • Correct location within atom	Missing/incorrect particles or location	
Electron Cloud	• Correct particle found here • Correct location within atom	Missing/incorrect particles or location	
Overall Appearance	• Easy to locate p+, n, e- • Easy to find nucleus • Easy to find electron cloud • Neat • Organized	1 part missing/incorrect	
Extra Special Features/Details	Be creative and be rewarded!		

© Mark Twain Media, Inc., Publishers

Everything Is Made of Atoms!

The atom is so small that it cannot be seen except under a very powerful microscope, but combine them, and they can form some powerful structures. The tallest building in the world, the Sears Tower, is made of mostly glass and steel; each of these substances is made of atoms.

For example, glass is made when silicon (Si) and oxygen (O) bond chemically to form SiO_2. This is the type of glass that is found in volcanic eruptions and is known as obsidian. The color of obsidian—black, green, or reddish—is due to contaminants that were present when it was formed. Today, glass is manufactured with certain specific properties in mind. It may need to be extra-strong or break without having sharp edges. Therefore, the glass has many compounds in its formula. Here is an example of the chemical composition of glass used for making bottles and windows.

Compound	Chemical Formula	Compound Name	% Composition	Material of Origin
Silica	SiO_2	Silicon dioxide	73.6	• Sand • Quartz
Soda	Na_2O	Sodium oxide	16.0	• Soda ash (Na_2CO_3) • Ashes of marine plants
Lime	CaO	Calcium oxide	5.2	• Chalk • Limestone ($CaCO_3$)
Potash	K_2O	Potassium oxide	0.6	• Ashes of inland plants
Magnesia	MgO	Magnesium oxide	3.6	• Impurity
Alumina	Al_2O_3	Aluminum oxide	1.0	• Impurity

There are 94 naturally occurring elements, and the tables below compare those elements with the percent of composition of the human body and the earth's crust.

Elements in the Human Body		
Oxygen	O	65.0 %
Carbon	C	18.5 %
Hydrogen	H	9.5 %
Nitrogen	N	3.3 %
Calcium	Ca	1.5 %
Sodium	Na	0.2 %
Potassium	K	0.4 %
Total		96.3 %

Elements in the Earth's Crust		
Oxygen	O	47.2 %
Silicon	Si	28.2 %
Aluminum	Al	8.2 %
Iron	Fe	5.1 %
Calcium	Ca	3.7 %
Sodium	Na	2.9 %
Potassium	K	2.6 %
Total		90.3 %

Do you notice some similarities? Do you notice some differences?

Learning About Atoms

Everything Is Made of Atoms! (cont.)

Name: _____ Date: _____

Next, you will find the elements and compounds that make up air. Remember, an element has its own box on the Periodic Table of the Elements, and a compound is made when two or more different types of atoms bond.

The chart below lists the components of air. The last two columns need to be completed; a few have already been done to show you just how easy the assignment is to complete.

Component	Symbol or Chemical Formula	Element or Compound?	If a compound, name the elements
a. Nitrogen	N	Element	
b. Oxygen	O		
c. Argon	Ar		
d. Carbon dioxide	CO_2	Compound	C, O
e. Neon	Ne		
f. Helium	He		
g. Krypton	Kr		
h. Sulfur dioxide	SO_2		
i. Methane	CH_4		
j. Hydrogen	H_2		
k. Nitrous oxide	N_2O		
l. Xenon	Xe		
m. Ozone	O_3		
n. Nitrogen dioxide	NO_2		
o. Iodine	I_2		
p. Carbon monoxide	CO		
q. Ammonia	NH_3		

Here are some fun facts about water and the elements and compounds found in it.

➡ Have you seen the hard, crusty, salt-like deposits on a faucet? The elements in tap water that make "hard water" deposits are calcium (Ca), manganese (Mn), and magnesium (Mg).

➡ Strong, rotten-egg odors in water indicate the presence of hydrogen sulfide (H_2S). This compound appears as a result of the decomposition of decaying underground organic deposits.

➡ Orange to red stains in your sink or bathtub are normally caused by iron (Fe) in the water.

➡ Blue to green stains in your sink or bathtub are usually caused by copper (Cu). If the pipes in your house are made of copper, this is usually the source of contamination.

© Mark Twain Media, Inc., Publishers

Atoms and the Periodic Table

Dmitri Mendeleev

A Russian physicist named Dmitri Mendeleev is credited with creating the Periodic Table of the Elements in the 1860s. Although many other scientists have made some important changes, the table allowed people to view the atoms in a pattern from smallest to largest and to recognize some common characteristics.

The modern Periodic Table is a table in which the elements are arranged in a pattern of increasing atomic number. Each line is read from left to right and starts over again when an energy level is full. There are many patterns to the Periodic Table. We will try to take it one step at a time with the goal of understanding and being able to use the information contained in the Periodic Table.

Let's start by reviewing the terms *atom* and *element*. Remember that an **atom** is the smallest particle of an element that has all the properties of that element. An **element** is made of two or more of the same kind of atom. So if I had mined a nugget of pure gold, I would have the element gold because all of the billions and billions of atoms making up the gold nugget are the atom gold. If I were able to look at just one gold atom under the world's most powerful electron microscope, I would see 79 protons. Gold is the only atom with 79 protons. If I counted 80 protons, I would have the atom mercury. Every proton looks the same; the number is what determines the atom. We know that gold and mercury are very different and yet very similar. Gold is yellowish in color and a solid at room temperature. Mercury, on the other hand, is silver in color and is the only metal that is a liquid at room temperature. The similarities are due to the fact that they are only one proton away from one another. They are both metals with heavy nuclei, are very shiny, and are very soft.

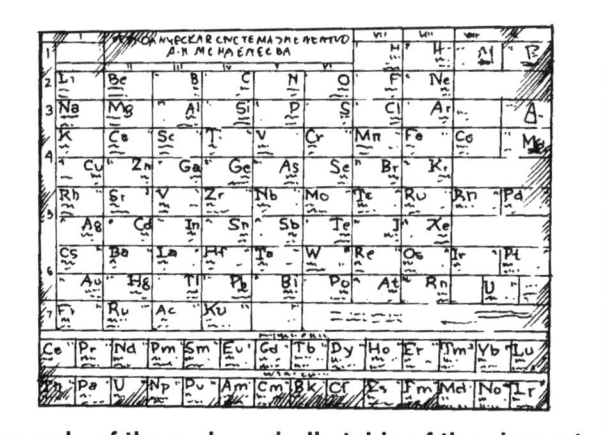
Example of the early periodic table of the elements

Most periodic tables give both the name of the element and the symbol used to represent the element. The symbols may be one, two, or three letters, and the first MUST be capitalized; if there is a second or third letter, they MUST be lowercase. The symbols used to represent the elements most often have a Latin origin, but some are also named for famous scientists.

Atoms and the Periodic Table (cont.)

Here are a few examples:

Element	Symbol	Name Origin
Carbon	C	Symbol from Latin: *carbo* (charcoal)
Copper	Cu	Symbol from Latin: *cuprum* (Island of Cyprus known for copper mines)
Mendelevium	Md	Named for Dmitri Mendeleev
Tungsten	W	Named from Swedish: *tung sten* (heavy stone) Symbol from German: tungsten is *wolfram*

The Periodic Table lists the elements according to increasing atomic number. Let's take a closer look at what this means. Hydrogen has one proton, so its atomic number is 1, while Helium has two protons, and its atomic number is 2. This is easy to understand, but when looking at the periodic table, we notice that they are on opposite sides of the table! We also see that Lithium has an atomic number of 3, which should position it next to Helium, but it appears as though Mendeleev decided to start a new line with Lithium ... so what's the deal? In order to understand these concepts, we need to discuss electrons and the electron cloud.

Do you recall the discussion of the fan blades representing the electron cloud, where they are spinning so fast that the path in which they are spinning becomes a blur? Well, let's slow the electrons down and look at the patterns they create. The first orbit closest to the nucleus is called the first energy level, and it can hold a maximum of two electrons. You must fill a level before moving out to the next energy level. The second energy level can hold a maximum of eight electrons. Energy levels 3 to 8 have differing numbers, so let's take a look at how to figure this out by looking at the periodic table. In some periodic tables, the electrons are shown in the electron distribution that shows you how the electrons are distributed in the electron cloud. In other periodic tables, there is no electron distribution listed, so you must look at the period. There are eight **periods**, and the energy levels are represented by period in the periodic table. A period is a horizontal row in the table.

Look at the periodic table. Period one represents the first energy level, which can hold up to two electrons. Now look at period 2. All of the elements in period 2 have electrons in two energy levels, and the second energy level can hold a maximum of eight electrons. If the element has more than 10 electrons (two in the first energy level + eight in the second), then you must start period 3 so that you have another energy level for the electrons. This placement of the elements continues throughout the table. We have learned enough for now, and it is time to do some practice.

Learning About Atoms

Atoms and the Periodic Table: Reinforcement Activity

Name: _____ Date: WED

Atoms and the Periodic Table: Reinforcement Activity

We are going to practice what has been discussed here with just the first 18 elements, because they seem to follow the rules better than the other elements. Carbon is given here as a key to read the table.

1st energy level write on Board
2nd energy level

Atomic Number | 6 | 2 | Electron Distribution
	4
C	
Carbon	

Period across

Period	1	2						13	14	15	16	17	18
1	1 H Hydrogen (1)												2 He Helium (2)
2	3 Li Lithium (2,1)	4 Be Beryllium (2,2)						5 B Boron (2,3)	6 C Carbon (2,4)	7 N Nitrogen (2,5)	8 O Oxygen (2,6)	9 F Fluorine (2,7)	10 Ne Neon (2,8)
3	11 Na Sodium (2,8,1)	12 Mg Magnesium (2,8,2)						13 Al Aluminum (2,8,3)	14 Si Silicon (2,8,4)	15 P Phosphorus (2,8,5)	16 S Sulfur (2,8,6)	17 Cl Chlorine (2,8,7)	18 Ar Argon (2,8,8)

Directions: Complete the following activity.

1. What is the symbol for Aluminum? __Al__

2. What is the atomic number for Aluminum? __13__

3. Aluminum has how many protons? __13__

4. Aluminum has how many electrons? __13__

5. What do you notice about the atomic number and the number of protons? __13 same__

6. What do you notice about the number of protons and the number of electrons? __13 same__

7. How many electrons does Aluminum have in the first energy level? __2__

review

Learning About Atoms

Atoms and the Periodic Table: Reinforcement Activity (cont.)

Review

8. When you add the electrons in each energy level, the sum represents the total number of __electrons__, which is the same as the number of __protons__ and the same as the __atomic__ __number__.

9. Aluminum has electrons in how many energy levels? __3__

10. Aluminum is in which period? __3__

11. What does the period tell you? __tells you the number of energy levels that contains electrons__

Complete the table below by using the information from the Periodic Table on the previous page.

Element	Symbol	Atomic Number	# of Protons	# of Electrons	# of Energy Levels	Period
Argon	Ar	18	18	18	3	3
Carbon	C	6	6	6	2	2
Helium	He	2	2	2	1	1
Lithium	Li	3	3	3	2	2
Oxygen	O	8	8	8	2	2
Sulfur	S	16	16	16	3	3
Silicon	Si	14	14	14	3	3
Sodium	Na	11	11	11	3	3

Groups and Periods

We know that the atomic number is the number of protons in the atom. But did you know that the atomic number is also said to "identify the atom"? This means that if the atomic number is 6, that means that it has 6 protons, and therefore, it could only be carbon. We also learned that the atomic number, the number of protons, and the number of electrons would always be the same for the elements of the periodic table. And lastly, we discussed the relationship between energy levels and the period in which an element is located.

Members of a period have their number of energy levels in common and that is about all. For example, if you look at any of the elements in period three, you will notice that each has a filled first energy level (2 e-) and a filled second energy level (8 e-). Now look at the third energy level, and you should see that it increases by one each time you move from left to right, with a maximum of eight electrons (e-) in the third energy level.

You already knew all of that, so let's move to groups. While **periods** run across, or horizontally, **groups** run down, or vertically, in the periodic table. Groups have many things in common; some physical and chemical properties are the same, and most importantly, the outermost energy level electrons are of the same number. Groups are numbered in many different ways. If you look at a complete periodic table, you will notice groups 1A to 8A and groups 3B to 7B, 7, and 1B to 2B. To avoid this confusion, some tables have the group columns labeled from 1 to 18. Groups numbered 1A to 8A correspond to group columns 1, 2, 13 to 18. These are called the main group elements because they follow the "rules" for electrons. Those in the middle, group columns 3 to 12 or 3B to 7B, 7, and 1B to 2B are called the "heavy metals" or "transition elements," and we will not be investigating them at this time. Now, I think you can see that following those systems for naming the group columns can be very confusing, so for our lessons we will skip the transition elements and number from left to right with those remaining.

Look at the table on the next page. It contains the same information as before, but now groups and atomic mass numbers have been added. Also, notice the gap between the columns representing Group 2 and Group 3. This space reminds you that the heavy metals or transition elements were removed from this periodic table.

Learning About Atoms   Groups and Periods

Name: _____ Date: _____

Groups and Periods (cont.)

```
Atomic   6        2   Electron
Number            4   Distribution
         C
         Carbon
         Mass Number
         12
```

Period	Group 1	Group 2	Group 3	Group 4	Group 5	Group 6	Group 7	Group 8
1	1, 1, H, Hydrogen, Mass # = 1							2, 2, He, Helium, Mass # = 4
2	3, 2/1, Li, Lithium, Mass # = 7	4, 2/2, Be, Beryllium, Mass # = 8	5, 2/3, B, Boron, Mass # = 11	6, 2/4, C, Carbon, Mass # = 12	7, 2/5, N, Nitrogen, Mass # = 14	8, 2/6, O, Oxygen, Mass # = 16	9, 2/7, F, Fluorine, Mass # = 19	10, 2/8, Ne, Neon, Mass # = 20
3	11, 2/8/1, Na, Sodium, Mass # = 23	12, 2/8/2, Mg, Magnesium, Mass # = 24	13, 2/8/3, Al, Aluminum, Mass # = 27	14, 2/8/4, Si, Silicon, Mass # = 28	15, 2/8/5, P, Phosphorus, Mass # = 31	16, 2/8/6, S, Sulfur, Mass # = 32	17, 2/8/7, Cl, Chlorine, Mass # = 35	18, 2/8/8, Ar, Argon, Mass # = 40

Look at group 1 elements. Do you notice that each element has 1 as the number of electrons in the outermost energy level in the electron distribution? Look at the group 6 elements. Do you notice that oxygen and sulfur both have six electrons in the outermost energy level? So now you are beginning to see the pattern. Let's add another vocabulary term—**valence electrons**. The valence electrons represent the electrons in the outermost energy level. That means that group 6 members have six valence electrons. Easy, right? Here are some practice problems you can do using the modified periodic table above.

Element	# of energy levels with electrons	Period in which element is located	# of valence electrons	Group in which element is located
Argon				
Carbon				
Helium *				
Lithium				
Silicon				
Sodium				

*Helium does not follow the group number rule, but the valence energy level is full.

© Mark Twain Media, Inc., Publishers

Learning About Atoms   Groups and Periods: Conclusions and Applications

Name: _____   Date: _____

Groups and Periods: Conclusions and Applications

Directions: Complete the following activity.

1. How can you predict an element's group? (What do group members have in common?)
   _____

2. How can you predict an element's period? (What do same-period members have in common?) _____

Element X has seven valence electrons located in the second energy level.

3. Element X's period is _____ and group is _____.

Chlorine has 17 electrons.

4. In what energy level will its outer electron(s) be located? _____
5. In what period will you find chlorine? _____
6. How many valence electrons does chlorine have? _____
7. In what group is chlorine located? _____

Element Y is located in group 3 and period 2.

8. In how many energy levels will you find electrons? _____
9. How many electrons are in its outer level? _____

Element Z has one valence electron located in the sixth energy level.

10. What is element Z's group _____ and period _____?
11. The number of valence electrons determines an element's _____.
12. The number of energy levels containing electrons determines the element's

    _____.

13. The periodic table is arranged by increasing _____ _____.
14. The atomic number represents the number of _____ and identifies the atom.
15. Members of a group have the same number of _____ _____.
16. Members of a period have the same number of _____ _____.
17. Groups run _____ or _____.
18. Periods run _____ or _____.

© Mark Twain Media, Inc., Publishers   19

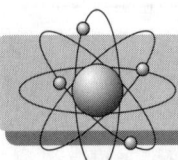

Element PowerPoint® Presentation

Every element on the periodic table has both unique and shared characteristics. In this project, you will be asked to look at one element in-depth and report on those characteristics and properties. The presentation is to be an oral report. You will use Microsoft PowerPoint® as the primary focal point or prompt for your project. There are many sources of information—for this project, you will be asked to reference both the Internet and books. Try to follow all of the steps carefully to end up with a completed project of which you can be proud and on which you can earn a great grade.

1. Join with your partner to select an element.

2. Study the rubric carefully and begin to gather information.

3. Check your spelling.

4. Be certain that the information presented in your PowerPoint® presentation is written in your own words. The easiest way to do this is to learn the information. In order to do this, you must gather the information from several reliable sources, read it for comprehension, and then write it so that it makes sense to you and to your audience.

5. You must first understand the information before presenting that information to the class. For example, if you write that aluminum is a ductile and malleable metal, you need to be able to explain what *ductile* and *malleable* mean when referring to aluminum.

6. Make your presentation exciting by adding visuals that enhance the information presented.

7. And lastly, when you present your element to the class, be organized, knowledgeable, and enthusiastic!

Learning About Atoms

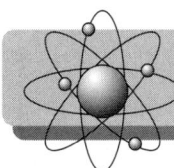

Rubric for Element PowerPoint® Presentation

Slide	20 Points	15 Points	10 Points	0 Points
#1 Introduction	1. Title 2. Student names 3. 1 or more relevant visuals 4. Correct spelling	1 area of slide either missing or incorrect	2 areas of slide either missing or incorrect	3 areas of slide either missing or incorrect
#2 Physical Properties	1. 4 or more physical properties 2. 1 or more relevant visuals 3. Correct spelling	1 area of slide either missing or incorrect	2 areas of slide either missing or incorrect	3 areas of slide either missing or incorrect
#3 Chemical Properties	1. 4 or more chemical properties 2. 1 or more relevant visuals 3. Correct spelling	1 area of slide either missing or incorrect	2 areas of slide either missing or incorrect	3 areas of slide either missing or incorrect
#4 Uses	1. 4 or more uses 2. 1 or more relevant visuals 3. Correct spelling	1 area of slide either missing or incorrect	2 areas of slide either missing or incorrect	3 areas of slide either missing or incorrect
#5 Credits	1. 1 or more Internet sites 2. 1 or more books 3. 1 or more relevant visuals 4. Correct spelling 5. Correct use of citations	1 area of slide either missing or incorrect	2 areas of slide either missing or incorrect	3 areas of slide either missing or incorrect
Oral Presentation	1. Voice heard by all 2. Expands/explains information on slides 3. Able to answer questions	1 area of presentation either missing, incorrect, or below expectations	2 areas of presentation either missing, incorrect, or below expectations	3 areas of presentation either missing, incorrect, or below expectations
Extra Credit	• Additional slides • Complex visuals • Other			

MLA and APA Source Cards

As the Internet develops, the manner in which citations are noted is constantly changing. These are the current acceptable ways to cite sources for your project.

MLA source card for an Internet site

Author (if given) _____

Title of article (if given) _____

Date of publication/posting _____

Organization/affiliation (if given) _____

Date you viewed the site (day mo yr.) _____

Internet address: <http:// _____>.

Example:
Mae, Thomas Lee. Elements for Life. Dec. 2000. Southern University, Thornfield, TX. 5 May 2003. <http://www.su.edu/~elements.htm>.

MLA source card for a book

Author(s) _____

Title _____

Editor (if any) _____

Edition (if not first, then 2nd ed., rev. ed.) _____

Place and date of publication _____

Publisher _____

Example:
Mae, T. and Tone, J. Everything Atoms. Boston: New Day Publishing, 2003.

MLA source card for a magazine/journal

Author(s) _____

Title _____

Title of the magazine/journal _____

Date of the issue the article appears _____

Pages on which the article appears _____

Example:
Mae, Thomas and Tone, Joshua. "Radioactive Elements and Reactivity." Journal of the New Frontier. 6 Dec. 2000: 11–22.

MLA and APA Source Cards (cont.)

APA source card for an Internet site

Author (if given) _____

Title of article (if given) _____

Date of publication/posting _____

Organization/affiliation (if given) _____

Date you viewed the site (day mo yr.) _____

Internet address: <http:// _____>.

Example:
   Mae, Thomas Lee. (Dec. 2000). <u>Elements for Life</u>. Retrieved May 5, 2003 from Southern University, Thornfield, TX. Website: http://www.su.edu/~elements.htm

APA source card for a book

Author(s) _____

Title _____

Editor (if any) _____

Edition (if not first, then 2nd ed., rev. ed.) _____

Place and date of publication _____

Publisher _____

Example:
   Mae, T. and Tone, J. (2003). <u>Everything Atoms</u>. Boston: New Day Publishing.

APA source card for a magazine/journal

Author(s) _____

Title _____

Title of the magazine/journal _____

Date of the issue the article appears _____

Pages on which the article appears _____

Example:
   Mae, T. and Tone, J. (2000, Dec. 16). Radioactive Elements and Reactivity. <u>Journal of the New Frontier</u>, 11–22.

Name: _____ Date: _____

Everything You Wanted to Know About Isotopes!

Isotope is very much a science-specific vocabulary word, and it means that an atom has extra neutrons or is missing some of its neutrons. This is not to be confused with ions, which are atoms missing or having extra electrons. Since the number of protons an atom contains determines the atom, neutron numbers can change, but the atom is still the same. Let's take a closer look at carbon and see if this makes sense.

Carbon is carbon because it has six protons. If the atom had seven protons, it would be nitrogen, and five protons would make the atom boron. Since carbon has six protons, we know that it also has six electrons (before it bonds). However, carbon atoms can be found with different numbers of neutrons. As you know, all living objects contain carbon, so carbon is found all over the universe. If the carbon comes from burning an oak tree in Illinois, we could analyze the carbon and find that it is made of six protons and six neutrons. This is named Carbon-12. The 12, as you can guess, is found by adding the number of protons and neutrons found in the nucleus of the atom. If we found some carbon from a rotting, decayed, and unidentifiable road kill in New Mexico and analyzed it, we might find that the carbon atoms all have six protons and eight neutrons. This would be Carbon-14. By referring to it as Carbon-12 or Carbon-14, you are telling the mass number of the carbon. The **mass number** is the sum of the protons and neutrons of the atom.

Let's go back to our original topic and review the term *isotope*. Carbon-12 and Carbon-14 are isotopes of carbon. It is true that these atoms are a little different, by two neutrons, but they are still carbon because they both still have six protons!

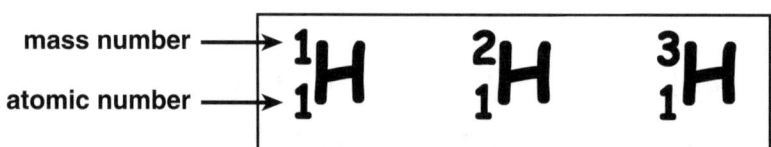

Here are three isotopes of hydrogen. Each atom of hydrogen has one proton in its nucleus, so the atomic number of each is "1." As you can see, the atomic number is the "1" listed to the bottom left of each "H." The **mass number** (the sum of the protons and neutrons) of each of these atoms varies due to the differing number of neutrons. The first isotope has one proton and zero neutrons. The second has one proton and one neutron. The third isotope of hydrogen contains one proton and two neutrons in the nucleus, for a total mass number of 3. The picture on the next page represents the three isotopes of hydrogen. These isotopes are so well known and used so often that scientists have named the isotopes of hydrogen.

Everything You Wanted to Know About Isotopes! (cont.)

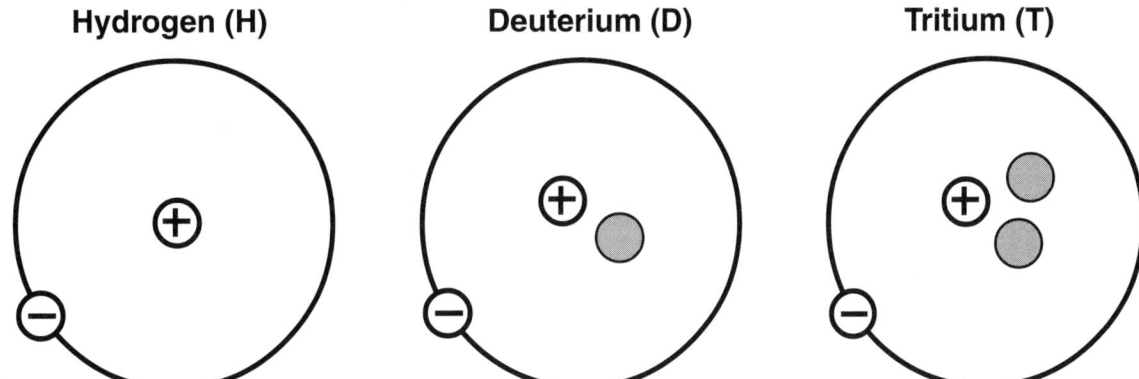

Isotopes seem to have a mind of their own and can't seem to follow any rules. So, of course, there are no set number of isotopes any one element can have. The best "balance" of protons and neutrons seems to do a better job of holding the nucleus together. There is a trend, however—light elements tend to have about as many neutrons as protons, and heavy elements tend to have more neutrons than protons. Atoms with too few or too many neutrons tend to be unstable. These atoms are radioactive. Their nuclei change or decay by giving off radiation in the form of particles or electromagnetic waves. (*FYI:* **Radiation** is energy that moves through space as wave particles, while **radioactivity** is the property of spontaneous release of radiation.)

Lastly, we need to understand the difference between mass number and atomic mass. We learned that mass number simply refers to the sum of the protons and neutrons. We use the mass number to identify the isotope. For example, chlorine has 17 protons, and one isotope of chlorine has 18 neutrons, while another common isotope has 20 neutrons. If we say chlorine-35, we are referring to the isotope with 18 neutrons (17 protons + 18 neutrons = 35 mass number).

Now let's take a look at the term **atomic mass**. If you look at a periodic table, you will notice that the atomic mass of an element is seldom a whole number. Here is an example of chlorine. The atomic mass is the average mass of an atom of an element. The atomic mass unit (amu) is defined as 1/12 the mass of a Carbon-12 atom. When atomic mass is calculated, all of the different isotopes of an atom are taken into account. If we take a closer look at chlorine, the atomic mass is 35.453. Basically, 75% of all chlorine is found as Chlorine-35, and 25% is Chlorine-37. If you take the average based on their mass numbers and percentage found, the atomic mass of chlorine is 35.453.

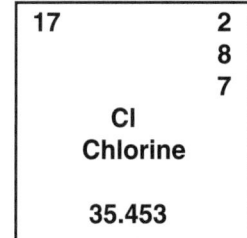

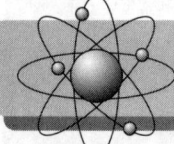

Isotopes: Reinforcement Activity

Name: _____ Date: _____

Directions: Complete the following table.

Atom	Symbol	# Protons	# Neutrons	Mass Number	Isotope Notation	Isotope Notation
Lithium	Li	3	4	7	$^{7}_{3}Li$	Li-7
Boron	B	5		11		
	N	7	6			
Magnesium			13	25		
Chlorine		17		35		
Chlorine		17		36		
Chlorine		17	20			
Calcium				40		
	Fe	26		56		
Copper		29		85		
Silver	Ag			108		
		79		197		
Lead		82	125			

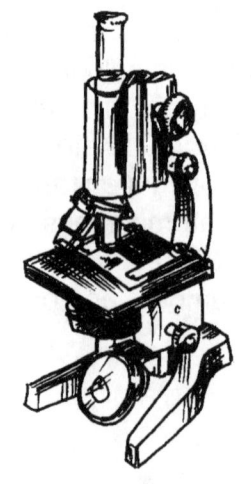

Isotopes: Reinforcement Activity (cont.)

Directions: Answer the following questions.

1. What is an isotope? _____

   _____

2. In the table on page 26, you found three isotopes of chlorine. Describe the differences in the three isotopes.

   _____

   _____

3. Compare the isotopes of light elements, lithium to calcium, with the heavier elements (iron to lead). Describe the major difference you notice.

   _____

   _____

   _____

4. When atoms have the best "balance" of protons and neutrons, the _____

   is more stable.

5. Describe radiation. _____

   _____

6. Describe radioactivity. _____

   _____

7. Describe mass number. _____

   _____

8. Describe atomic mass. _____

   _____

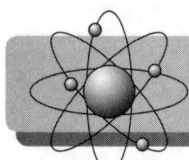

Carbon Dating

What is carbon dating?

We have all heard of carbon dating when someone is discussing the date of something very old, such as an artifact from a tomb or the Shroud of Turin. Basically, we use the decay rate of Carbon-14 to tell us when something stopped living. Since all living things contain carbon, the decay of carbon takes place when something dies; therefore, we have a place to start. Let's get a little more scientific and look at what we know about carbon and isotopes.

Carbon is found in the chemical make-up of all living things. Plants will acquire carbon dioxide in the photosynthesis process, and this carbon is passed to any organism that eats the plant. Most carbon found in living things has 12 protons, and this would be the isotope Carbon-12. Each living organism also contains some Carbon-13 and Carbon-14. As soon as an organism dies, it no longer takes in new Carbon-12, Carbon-13, or Carbon-14. Carbon-12 is stable and does not break apart, but Carbon-14 is unstable or radioactive. Another interesting factor is that the percentage of C-12, C-13, and C-14 is the same for all living organisms. In case you are interested, the percentages are:

$$\begin{array}{ll} \text{Carbon-12} & 98.89\% \\ \text{Carbon-13} & 1.11\% \\ \text{Carbon-14} & 0.00000000010\% \end{array}$$

Or you may want to think of it as a ratio. For every one Carbon-14 atom in nature, there are 1,000,000,000,000 Carbon-12 atoms (one in a trillion).

When the organism dies, the Carbon-14 begins a constant and predictable decay to Nitrogen-14. Remember that the number of protons determines the atom, and carbon has 6 protons. As it decays, carbon (with 6 protons) becomes nitrogen (with 5 protons). This predictable change in the ratio of C-14 to C-12 (1:1,000,000,000,000) helps scientists to determine the date of the object.

Carbon Decay

Carbon-12 does not decay and therefore is not radioactive. The amount of C-12 in an object that is no longer living remains the same as when the object died. Carbon-14 is radioactive and does decay. To **decay** means to break down or break apart. C-14 decays spontaneously (without being told to decay) and continuously. Carbon-14 decays to Nitrogen-14. It takes about 5,730 years for **half** of the C-14 to decay to N-14. In another 5,730 years, half of the half that was left will decay and so on. This allows us to track the decay for about 50,000 to 70,000 years with fairly good accuracy. Here is another way to look at the decay rate. If you have 100 atoms of C-14 in the year 2000 and the half-life is 10 years (we know it is 5,730 but 10 years is easier to imagine), then in 2010, you will have 50 atoms of C-14. In the year 2020, another half-life will pass, and there will be 25 atoms of C-14 remaining. Look at the following chart for a closer look.

Carbon Dating (cont.)

Year	Atoms of C-14
2000	100
2010	50
2020	25
2030	12.5
2040	6.25
2050	3.125
2060	1.5625
2070	0.78125
2080	0.390625
2090	0.1953125

As you can see by the sixth, seventh, and eighth half-life, there is very little C-14 left, and so its usefulness has diminished as well. This is why carbon dating is only useful for objects dating back about 50,000 years (8 half-lives).

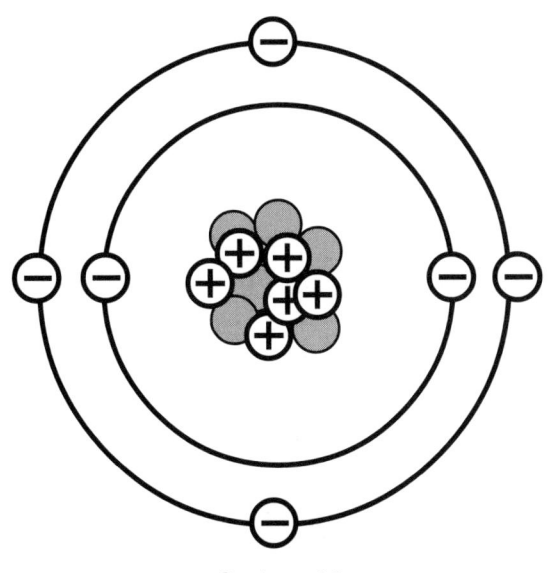

Carbon-12

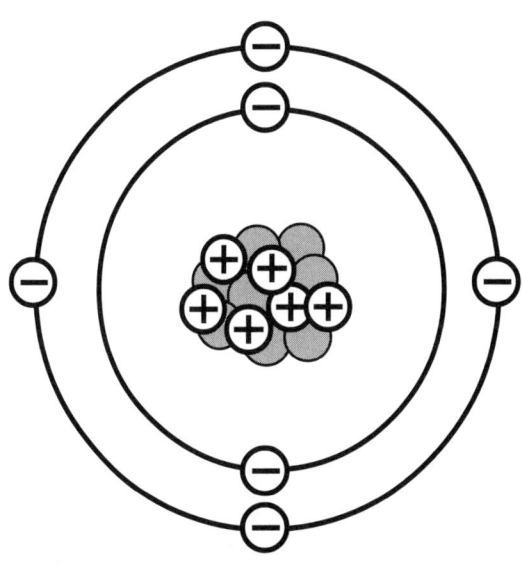

Carbon-14

Learning About Atoms   The Isotopes of Pennies: Activity and Investigation

Name: _____ Date: _____

The Isotopes of Pennies: Activity and Investigation

1. An isotope is _____
   _____

2. Two isotopes of carbon are C-12 and C-14. What does C-12 mean, and how does it compare to C-14?
   _____
   _____
   _____

3. Define average atomic mass. _____
   _____

   Now that we have reviewed isotopes, why don't we look at the pennies you carry around in your pocket? Pretend the penny is an atom, and let's see if there are some isotopes of penny.

A. Gather 20 pennies and find their mass (be very careful to be accurate).
B. Put those pennies in a pile and gather another group of 20 pennies and find their mass.
C. Record the masses in the following data table.

Group	Mass of 20 pennies	# of pennies dated before 1982	# pennies dated 1982 to present
# 1	g		
# 2	g		

D. Do you think there is a difference in the masses of the pennies dated before 1982? Of course you can infer that from the data you collected. Complete the following table to gather some raw data to help you understand your data gathered in the first table.

Date penny minted	Mass of 20 pennies	Average Mass of one penny (mass / 20)
Before 1982	g	g
1982–present	g	g

© Mark Twain Media, Inc., Publishers

Learning About... The Isotopes of Pennies: Activity and Investigation

Name: _____ Date: _____

The Isotopes of Pennies: Activity and Investigation (cont.)

E. Explain why your group 1 pennies have a different mass than your group 2 pennies.

_____

_____

F. How many isotopes of the penny atoms did you find? _____ Explain your answer.

_____

_____

In 1982, the United States government changed the way it minted pennies. Copper was becoming more expensive, so they changed the chemical composition. Prior to 1982, pennies were made of a material containing 95% copper and 5% tin. Since 1982, our pennies have a zinc core with a copper coating. This is a drastic change, and you can see how that change affected the mass of the penny.

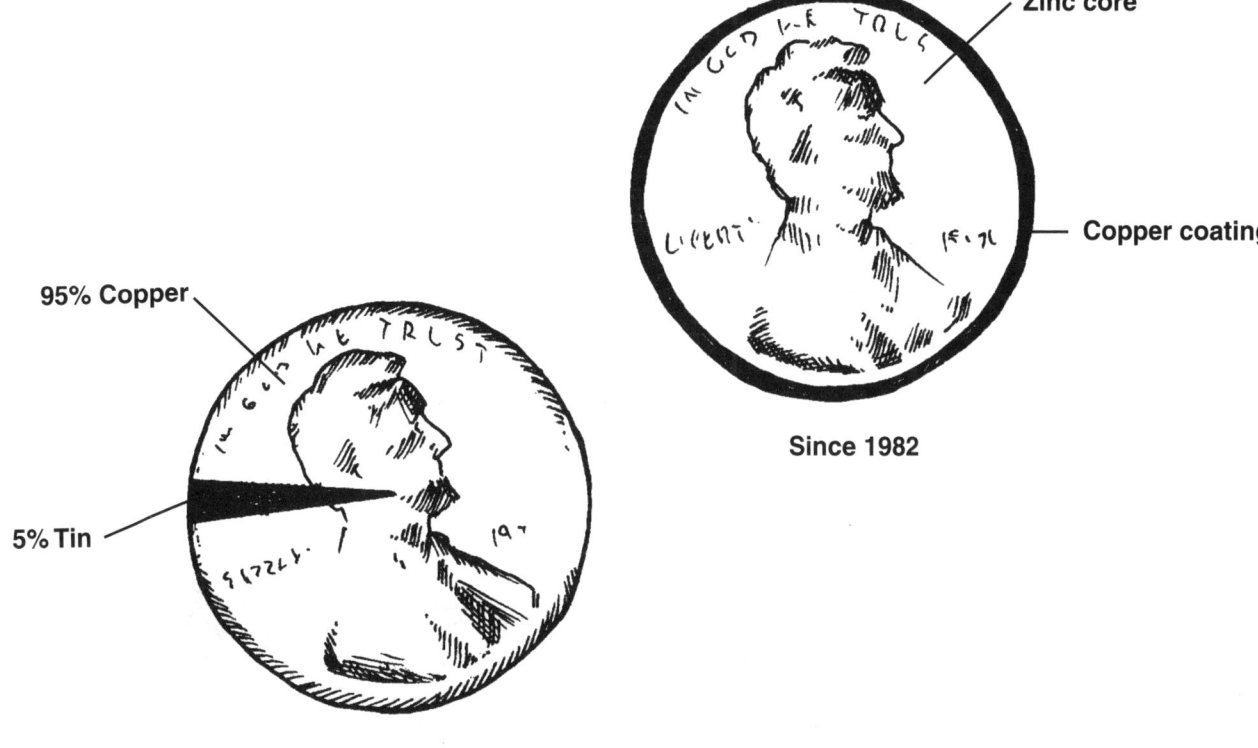

Since 1982 — Zinc core, Copper coating

Before 1982 — 95% Copper, 5% Tin

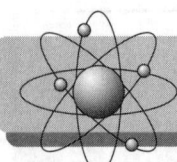
Uses of Carbon Dating

Carbon dating is being used to date all sorts of living things. Because the ratio of C-14 to C-12 is constant and the decay of C-14 is both spontaneous and constant, this method of measurement can be used worldwide with accuracy and uniformity.

The four factors affecting accurate dating using Carbon-14 are:
1. Objects that did not get their carbon from the air
2. Objects that were formed from a mixture of objects
3. Objects that were tested after the 1970s when C-14 dating became more accurate
4. Objects that are too young and possibly contaminated with excessive amounts of C-14

A closer look at the above four factors will help you to understand the problems.
- *Factor 1* refers to objects that did not acquire their carbon from the air but rather from rocks. Since C-14 is created in the upper atmosphere, rocks do not have this C-14. The objects may be sea creatures, petroleum products, etc.
- *Factor 2* refers to objects that were formed when several objects were mixed to create a new object. This creates a "contaminated" sample.
- *Factor 3* refers to objects tested up to 1970. The testing was not as accurate due to advances in instrumentation, tree ring calibration as the constant rather than the sun, and better methods to detect contamination.
- *Factor 4* refers to "human" influences. In the 1950s, nuclear tests, nuclear bombs, and nuclear power plants created a lot of C-14 in the air, disrupting the one in a trillion ratio of C-14 to C-12. Another "human" factor affecting the ratio is the burning of fossil fuels, which contains C-12 but not C-14.

Can something older than 50,000 years be dated?

We have learned that Carbon-14 can be used to date objects up to 50,000 to 70,000 years old. Using the knowledge you have about how Carbon-14 dating works, it would seem that to date something older than 70,000 years old, we would need a radioactive atom with a half-life that is much longer. Guess what? Scientists have found these atoms. Check out this table that shows half-lives.

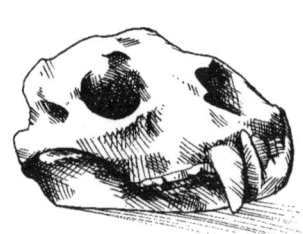

Radioactive Atom	Half life
Rubidium-87	48.8 billion years
Potassium-40	1.25 billion years
Uranium-235	704 million years
Technetium-99m	6 hours

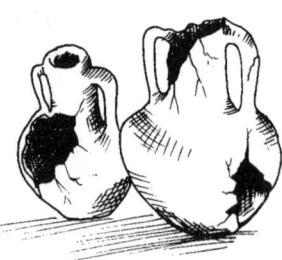

Carbon Dating: Reinforcement Activity

1. What is carbon dating? _____

2. Explain the differences between Carbon-12, Carbon-13, and Carbon-14.

3. Where is Carbon-14 made? _____

4. How does carbon get into living things? _____

5. After about the eighth half-life of C-14, we are no longer confident that the dating is accurate and generally do not use it past 50,000 years. Why is this?

Directions: Fill in the blanks below with the words in the word bank.

Carbon-12	decayed	Uranium-235	carbon dating in the 1950s
Carbon-14	50,000	half-life	ocean or sea objects
Nitrogen-14	nuclear testing	ratio of C-14 to C-12	

6. The _____ is one in a trillion.

7. All living organisms contain 98.89% _____, 1.11% Carbon-13, and 0.00000000010% _____.

8. In the 1950s, _____ released Carbon-14 into the air and disrupted the C-14:C-12 ratio.

9. When Carbon-14 decays, _____ is produced.

10. _____ was not accurate due to poor measurement.

11. When a radioactive element breaks down or breaks apart, we say that it has _____.

12. The _____ of Carbon-14 is about 5,730 years.

13. Objects that have not acquired carbon from the air, such as _____ _____, are not able to be dated by the carbon dating method.

14. Objects that are up to about _____ years old can be dated using the decay of Carbon-14.

15. _____ has a half-life of 704 million years and can be used to date some rocks and fossils.

Name: _____ Date: _____

Radioactive Decay of the Penny: Activity and Investigation

Papertearium

First, we are going to look at a piece of paper as a radioactive element.

Recall that a half-life is the time it takes for half of the element to decay. The half-life of "papertearium" is 15 seconds. We will decay papertearium for eight to 10 half-lives.

Start with a sheet of notebook paper; this will represent our element papertearium with a half-life of 15 seconds.

In 15 seconds, the teacher will say the first half-life has ended. At this point, you will tear the paper in half and drop one of the halves onto your desk and keep the other half.

In 15 seconds, the teacher will say the second half-life has ended, and you will again tear the paper in half and drop one of the halves onto your desk and keep the other half.

This procedure will be repeated every 15 seconds until the eighth, ninth, or tenth half-life has been called or until you are no longer able to tear the paper in half.

What half-life were you able to reach and still have a very, very small amount of the element papertearium?

Carbon-14 has a half-life of 5,730 years, and we learned that we could accurately date an object back about 50,000 years. If we were using papertearium to find the half-life of an object, how far out (number of seconds) would we be able to accurately measure the date of the object's death?

Lincolnium

Next, we are going to look at the decay as being fairly predictable, even though we are going to play a game of chance.

1. Place exactly 100 pennies in a container or box. Each of these pennies represents the element Lincolnium. (Also an imaginary element named for Lincoln's head, which is found on each of the pennies!)

2. Shake the container, and when you open it, you will see that some of Mr. Lincoln's heads have changed to the Lincoln Monument!

3. Remove all the pennies that show the Lincoln Monument.

4. Count and record the number removed after each shake.

5. Continue until no pennies remain in the container.

Radioactive Decay of the Penny: Activity and Investigation (cont.)

Half-life	# Pennies	# Pennies expected to be removed this shake	% Pennies left	Pennies left as fractions
1st		50	50%	1/2
2nd		25	25%	1/4
3rd		13	13%	1/8
4th		6	6%	1/16
5th		3	3%	1/32
6th		1	1%	1/64
7th		0	0%	1/128
8th				
9th				
10th				

1. In a half-life, you should expect to find that _____ of the radioactive element has decayed.

2. Did your results come close to this expectation in your test? _____

3. To which half-life of Lincolnium would you be able to date an object and feel confident of the results? _____

4. Defend your answer using your data above. _____

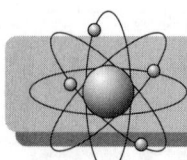

Famous Scientist Report

Scientific understandings involve both the actual concept and the understandings and events that shaped the development of that concept. The concept of the atom was first thought of many years ago and is ongoing today. As we take a closer look at the people who helped us understand the atom, we will find that they followed the same scientific experimentation model we use in our own classroom.

- **Questions:** Each scientist wondered how something worked or acted.

- **Background Information:** Each scientist gathered the necessary background information to help answer his/her questions.

- **Experimentation:** Each scientist tried to find a reasonable answer to the question that plagued his/her thoughts.

- **Misinformation, incorrect thoughts, and failed experiments:** Each scientist made wrong turns and had failed ideas on his/her way to a new understanding.

- **Sharing Discoveries:** Each scientist shared his/her work so that others could be helped to understand the concept that was plaguing him/her.

You will be asked to pick a scientist who helped us understand what we know about atoms. A great number of these scientists were talked about in "The History of the Atom." Next, you will be asked to find out how the scientist came to his/her discovery, and then you will share what you have learned.

The Research
You will need to research the following information for your presentation:
- ✔ Scientist's name
- ✔ Questions
- ✔ Background information to help us understand the scientist
- ✔ Background information that helped the scientist with his/her discovery
- ✔ How did he/she conduct his/her experiment?
- ✔ What problems did he/she encounter when trying to understand his/her discovery?
- ✔ What was the discovery or understanding of your famous scientist?

The Sharing of your Research
- ✔ You will be asked to role-play your scientist by giving an oral presentation "in character."
- ✔ Introduce yourself. (Pretend you are the scientist!)
- ✔ Tell us who you are by sharing the time and something about you that has caused you to become a scientist.
- ✔ Ask the questions of the class that you were asking of yourself and your colleagues when you were about to make your discovery.
- ✔ Tell us what information you had that led you to conduct your experiments.
- ✔ Explain some of your experiments.
- ✔ Lastly, tell us what discovery you made that caused you to become such a famous scientist.

Learning About Atoms

Name: _____ Date: _____

Research a Famous Scientist

Directions: Use this sheet as a guide for information to include in your presentation.

Name of scientist: _____

When and where did the scientist live? _____
_____

What interesting information do we need to know to better understand this scientist (education, influential persons in his/her life, obstacles he/she overcame ...)?
_____
_____
_____

What question was the scientist trying to answer? _____
_____
_____

What information did the scientist have that led to the question he/she was trying to answer?
_____
_____

How did the scientist conduct his/her experiment? _____
_____
_____

What problems did the scientist encounter when trying to understand his/her discovery?
_____
_____

What was the discovery or understanding of your famous scientist?
_____
_____
_____

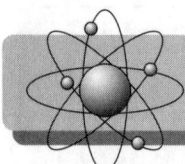

Atoms Vocabulary

atom: The simplest form of matter that cannot be changed into a simpler form by ordinary means; building block of matter

atomic mass unit (amu): 1/12 the mass of a Carbon-12 atom

atomic mass: the average mass of an element; found by averaging all the different isotopes of an element

atomic number: the number of protons in an atom; this number identifies the atom

compound: a substance made of two or more different kinds of atoms

decay: to break down or break apart

electron: the part of the atom with a negative charge; located in the electron cloud orbiting the nucleus

element: a substance made of many of the same kind of atom

group: elements listed in a vertical column on the periodic table that all have the same number of valence electrons

half-life: the time it takes for half of the radioactive atoms in a substance to decay

isotope: an element with different numbers of neutrons than protons

mass number: the sum of the protons and neutrons of an atom

matter: anything that has mass and takes up space

neutron: the part of the atom with no charge or a neutral charge; located in the nucleus

nucleus: central part of the atom where the protons and neutrons are found

period: elements listed in a horizontal row on the periodic table that all have the same number of energy levels

periodic table of the elements: a chart organized to show elements by increasing atomic number

proton: the part of the atom with a positive charge; located in the nucleus

radiation: energy that moves through space as wave particles

radioactivity: the property of spontaneous and continuous release of radiation

symbol: shortened way of representing the different atoms, consisting of one, two, or three letters

valence electrons: the electrons in the outermost energy level of an atom

Atoms Crossword Puzzle

Directions: Complete the crossword puzzle using the clues below and the information you have learned about atoms in this unit.

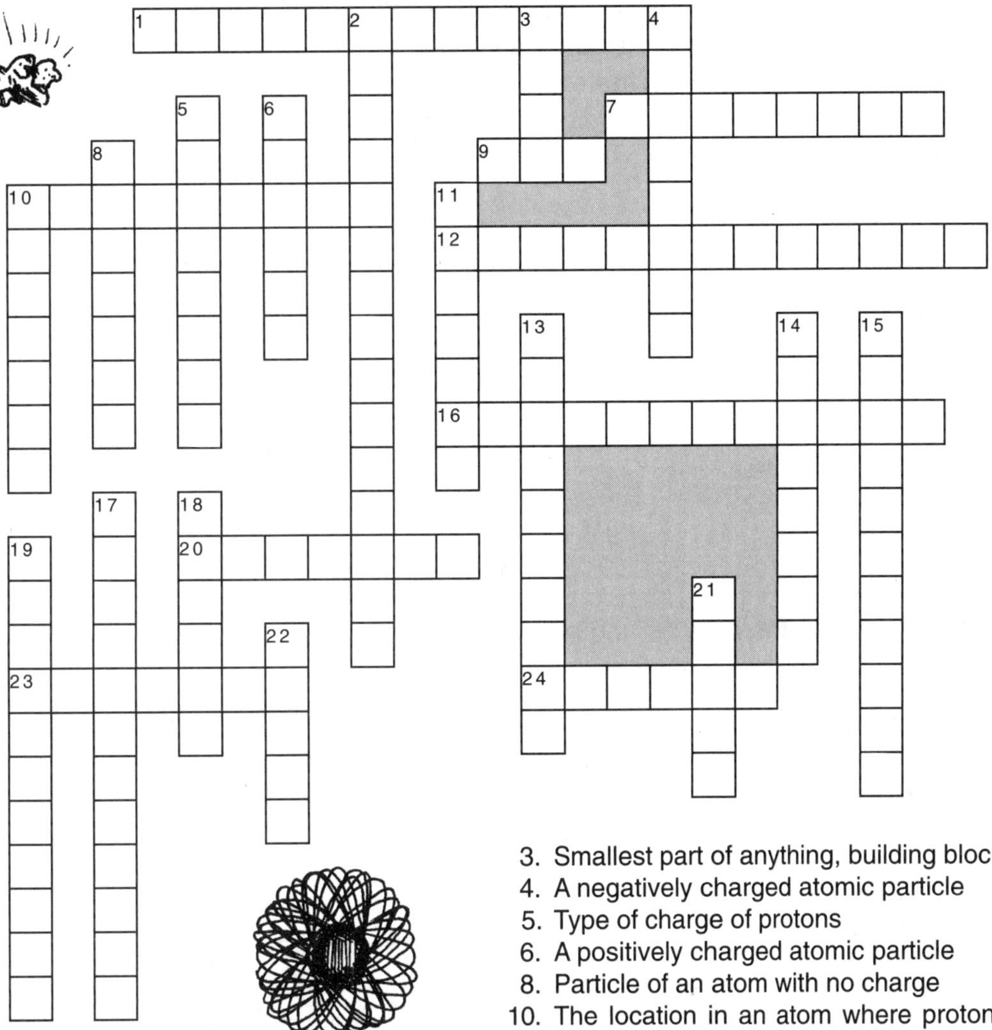

ACROSS
1. Arrangement of atoms by increasing atomic number (two words)
7. The charge of the electrons
9. Abbreviation for atomic mass unit
10. Created the first accepted model of the atom (two words)
12. The location in the atom where electrons are found (two words)
16. Identifies the atom, number of protons (two words)
20. Many of all of the same type of atom
23. Atom with a different number of neutrons than protons
24. One, two, or three letters used to represent an atom

DOWN
2. The creator of the periodic table (two words)
3. Smallest part of anything, building block of matter
4. A negatively charged atomic particle
5. Type of charge of protons
6. A positively charged atomic particle
8. Particle of an atom with no charge
10. The location in an atom where protons and neutrons are found
11. Type of charge of the neutrons
13. The sum of the protons and neutrons of an atom (two words)
14. Substance made of two or more different types of atoms
15. Area in an electron cloud where electrons are found (two words)
17. Method used to find the age of an organism using the decay of Carbon-14 (two words)
18. Elements that have the same number of energy levels
19. Atoms that have the ability to spontaneously and continuously decay
21. Elements that have the same number of valence electrons
22. Breaking down or breaking apart

Learning About Atoms

Jeopardy! Review Game

Teacher Directions: Photocopy the sets of answers and questions and glue or tape each one to an index card. On the front of the card, write the point value of the question. Have the students group the cards according to point value. Each group can choose any point value and the opposing team will read the answer and wait for the question response. If correct, record the points, and then give the other team their turn. Keep this going until all cards have been used or time is up. This game is lots of fun, and by making a set of questions for each group of 4 students, everyone gets to participate and ready themselves for the test.

10-Point Questions

A: The part of the atom with a negative charge. **Q:** What is an electron? 10	**A:** The part of the atom with a positive charge. **Q:** What is a proton? 10
A: The smallest part of matter. **Q:** What is an atom? 10	**A:** The part of the atom with no charge or a neutral charge. **Q:** What is a neutron? 10
A: This is the location of the protons and neutrons. **Q:** Where is the nucleus? 10	**A:** This is the location of the electrons. **Q:** Where is in the electron cloud? 10

20-Point Questions

A: A shortened way to represent the atoms. **Q:** What is a symbol? 20	**A:** Members of this are all the same kind of atom. **Q:** What is an element? 20
A: The number of protons identifies the atom and tells this. **Q:** What is the atomic number? 20	**A:** This is a chart organized to show elements by increasing atomic number. **Q:** What is the periodic table? 20
A: amu **Q:** What is the abbreviation for Atomic Mass Unit? 20	**A:** This shows where the electrons are located within the electron cloud. **Q:** What are the energy levels? 20
A: Members all have the same number of valence electrons. **Q:** What is a group? 20	**A:** Members all have the same number of energy levels. **Q:** What is a period? 20

Jeopardy! Review Game (cont.)

30-Point Questions

A: The number of neutrons can change. **Q:** How do isotopes differ? 30	**A:** 5,730 years **Q:** What is the half-life of Carbon-14? 30
A: This is the method used to determine the age of objects up to 50,000 years old. **Q:** What is carbon dating? 30	**A:** The ratio of C-14 to C-12. **Q:** What is one in a trillion? 30
A: This is the scientist who proposed the first widely accepted model of the atom. **Q:** Who is Niels Bohr? 30	**A:** This process is spontaneous and continuous for radioactive elements. **Q:** What is decay? 30
A: This is made of two or more elements chemically bonded. **Q:** What is a compound? 30	**A:** The electron is this much smaller than the protons and neutrons. **Q:** What is 1,800 times smaller? 30

40-Point Questions

A: This is the isotope of hydrogen containing 2 neutrons. **Q:** What is Tritium? 40	**A:** To date, this is the number of different naturally occurring atoms. **Q:** What are 94? 40
A: The elements nitrogen, oxygen, and argon make up this percentage of air. **Q:** What is 99.9%? 40	**A:** This is the composition of pennies minted from 1982 to the present. 40 **Q:** What is a zinc core covered with copper?
A: This is found when you add all of the naturally occurring isotopes for an element. **Q:** What is atomic mass? 40	**A:** This is the composition of pennies minted prior to 1982. **Q:** What is 95% copper and 5% tin? 40
A: This element was named for the Latin term *cuprum*. **Q:** What is copper? 40	**A:** These are the atoms created in the lab and not found in nature. **Q:** What are synthetic atoms? 40

Atoms Unit Test

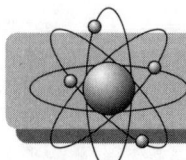

I. Multiple Choice: Write the letter of the correct answer on the line to the left of the question.

_____ 1. What is an atom?
   a. the smallest part of anything
   b. a composite of lots of things
   c. something that is radioactive
   d. something only made in the laboratory

_____ 2. An element is _____.
   a. only found in nature
   b. many of the same kind of atom
   c. only found in the laboratory
   d. many different kinds of atoms

_____ 3. The atomic number tells _____.
   a. how an atom reacts to heat
   b. the number of electron clouds for an element
   c. if an atom is radioactive
   d. the number of protons in an atom

_____ 4. The chart of the elements was developed many years ago by a famous Russian physicist named Dmitri Mendeleev. The name of this chart is the _____ table.
   a. Mendeleev
   b. properties
   c. chemical activities
   d. periodic

_____ 5. Atoms of the same element with different numbers of neutrons are called _____.
   a. transition elements
   b. metalloids
   c. isotopes
   d. ions

_____ 6. The center of an atom where the protons and neutrons are found is the _____.
   a. epicenter
   b. nucleus
   c. core
   d. cloud

_____ 7. Two isotopes of carbon are Carbon-12 and Carbon-14. How do these isotopes differ?
   a. by two protons
   b. by two neutrons
   c. by two electrons
   d. by two atoms

II. Shared Answers: You may use answers *a, b,* and *c* more than once.

_____ 8. The _____ has a positive charge.   **a. proton**
_____ 9. This particle is found in the electron cloud.   **b. neutron**
_____ 10. The _____ has a negative charge.   **c. electron**
_____ 11. This particle has no charge.
_____ 12. This particle is found in the nucleus and is the same as the atomic number.
_____ 13. This particle is found in the nucleus and can be used to determine the isotope.

Learning About Atoms

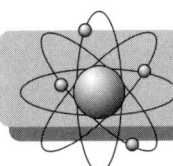 # Atoms Unit Test (cont.)

III. Matching: Put the letter of the phrase in the space next to the word it matches.

_____ 1. amu
_____ 2. symbol
_____ 3. periodic table
_____ 4. group
_____ 5. period
_____ 6. valence electrons
_____ 7. energy level
_____ 8. element
_____ 9. atomic mass
_____ 10. isotopes of carbon
_____ 11. carbon dating
_____ 12. radioactive
_____ 13. half-life
_____ 14. synthetic atoms

a. electrons in the outermost energy level of the electron cloud
b. many of all of the same kind of atom
c. arrangement of atoms by increasing atomic number
d. levels in electron cloud where electrons are found
e. atoms having the ability to spontaneously decay
f. C-12, C-13, and C-14
g. atomic mass unit
h. members have the same number of valence electrons
i. atoms created in the lab and not found in nature
j. one, two, or three letters used to represent an atom
k. time it takes for half of a radioactive isotope to decay
l. members have the same number of energy levels
m. sum of the protons and the neutrons of an atom
n. method used to find the age of a dead organism

IV. Short Answer: Describe how radioactive C-14 can be used to date an item.

Here is a list of words and phrases that you may want to use.

radioactive	5,730 years	C-14 present at time of death
decay	isotopes	ocean or sea objects
half-life	50,000 years	one to a trillion

_____
_____
_____
_____
_____
_____

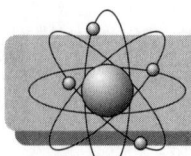

References Page

MLA Style

MLA Style. 2001-2003. Modern Language Association of America, 26 June 2003.

<http://www.mla.org/>.

A Guide for Writing Research Papers: MLA Style. June 12, 2002. Capital Community College, Hartford, CT. 26 June 2003.

<http://webster.commnet.edu/mla/index.shtml>

APA Style

APA Online. Retrieved June 26, 2003 from American Psychological Association. Website: http://www.apastyle.org/

Burgess, Patricia S. (1995). *A Guide for Writing Research Papers: APA Style.* Retrieved June 26, 2003 from Capital Community College, Hartford, CT. Website: http://webster.commnet.edu/apa/apa_index.htm

Elements in Human Body and Earth's Crust

Campbell, N., Mitchell, L.G., and Reece, J.B. (2000). *Biology Concepts and Connections.* 3rd ed. San Francisco: Addison Wesley Longman, p.19.

Composition of Silica Glass

Corning Museum of Glass. Retrieved June 26, 2003. Corning, NY. Website: http://www.cmog.org/

Textbook References

Physical Science. Glencoe/McGraw-Hill, 1997.

Discover the Wonder. Scott Foresman Science, 2000.

Discovery Works. Houghton Mifflin, 2003.

Answer Keys

Matter and the Atom: Reinforcement Activity (p. 5)
Student Observer: An atom is the smallest part of matter.
Analyze: Everything is made of matter, and all matter is made of atoms.
1. 94
2. 25 (at this printing)
3. Naturally occurring atoms are those found in nature; synthetic atoms are made in the lab.
4. Matter is what everything is made of, and all matter is made of atoms.
5. Many of the same kind of atom
6. Matter can be made of many different kinds of atoms, while an element is made of many of the same atom.
7. Atoms are the smallest part of anything, and an element must contain two or more of the same atom.

The Parts of the Atom: Reinforcement Activity (p. 8)
Student Observer: The parts of an atom include the proton, neutron, and electron.
Analyze: Models help us understand the atom by visualizing something we already know something about.
1. three
2. protons, neutrons, and electrons
3. nucleus
4. electron cloud
5. orbit
6. protons and neutrons
7. electrons
8. positive (+)
9. none, neutral
10. negative (-)
11. 6
12. 6
13. 6
14. 12 amu
15. empty space

Everything Is Made of Atoms! (p. 12)
Answers to components of air chart
b. Oxygen: element
c. Argon: element
e. Neon: element
f. Helium: element
g. Krypton: element
h. Sulfur dioxide: compound; S, O
i. Methane: compound; C, H
j. Hydrogen: element
k. Nitrous oxide: compound; N, O
l. Xenon: element
m. Ozone: element (oxygen)
n. Nitrogen dioxide: compound; N, O
o. Iodine: element
p. Carbon monoxide: compound; C, O
q. Ammonia: compound; N, H

Atoms and the Periodic Table: Reinforcement Activity (p. 15–16)
1. Al
2. 13
3. 13
4. 13
5. The atomic number and number of protons are the same.
6. The number of protons and electrons are the same.
7. 2
8. electrons, protons, atomic number
9. 3
10. 3
11. The period tells the number of energy levels containing electrons.

Element	Symbol	Atomic Number	# of Protons	# of Electrons	# of Energy Levels	Period
Argon	Ar	18	18	18	3	3
Carbon	C	6	6	6	2	2
Helium	He	2	2	2	1	1
Lithium	Li	3	3	3	2	2
Oxygen	O	8	8	8	2	2
Sulfur	S	16	16	16	3	3
Silicon	Si	14	14	14	3	3
Sodium	Na	11	11	11	3	3

Groups and Periods Practice (p. 18)

Element	# of energy levels with electrons	Period in which element is located	# of valence electrons	Group in which element is located
Argon	3	3	8	8
Carbon	2	2	4	4
Helium *	1	1	2	8
Lithium	2	2	1	1
Silicon	3	3	4	4
Sodium	3	3	1	1

Groups and Periods: Conclusions and Applications (p. 19)
1. Each group member has the same number of valence electrons.
2. Each period member has the same number of energy levels containing electrons.
3. 2, 7
4. third
5. 3
6. 7
7. 7
8. 2
9. 3
10. 1, 6
11. group
12. period
13. atomic number
14. protons
15. valence electrons
16. energy levels
17. down or vertically
18. across or horizontally

Learning About Atoms — Answer Keys

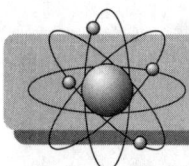

Isotopes: Reinforcement Activity (p. 26–27)

Atom	Symbol	# Protons	# Neutrons	Mass Number	Isotope Notation	Isotope Notation
Lithium	Li	3	4	7	$^{7}_{3}Li$	Li-7
Boron	B	5	6	11	$^{11}_{5}B$	B-11
Nitrogen	N	7	6	13	$^{13}_{7}N$	N-13
Magnesium	Mg	12	13	25	$^{25}_{12}Mg$	Mg-25
Chlorine	Cl	17	18	35	$^{35}_{17}Cl$	Cl-35
Chlorine	Cl	17	19	36	$^{36}_{17}Cl$	Cl-36
Chlorine	Cl	17	20	37	$^{37}_{17}Cl$	Cl-37
Calcium	Ca	20	20	40	$^{40}_{20}Ca$	Ca-40
Iron	Fe	26	30	56	$^{56}_{26}Fe$	Fe-56
Copper	Cu	29	56	85	$^{85}_{29}Cu$	Cu-85
Silver	Ag	47	61	108	$^{108}_{47}Ag$	Ag-108
Gold	Au	79	118	197	$^{197}_{79}Au$	Au-197
Lead	Pb	82	125	207	$^{207}_{82}Pb$	Pb-207

1. an element with different numbers of neutrons
2. the number of neutrons was different
3. The number of neutrons was varied more for the heavier elements.
4. nucleus
5. energy that moves through space
6. property of spontaneous release of radiation
7. the sum of protons and neutrons
8. the average of mass number for all of the isotopes of an element

The Isotopes of Pennies: Activity and Investigation (p. 30–31)

1. An isotope is an element with different numbers of neutrons.
2. C-12 means that this isotope of carbon contains 6 protons and 6 neutrons, thus C-12.
   C-14 contains 6 protons and 8 neutrons of carbon, thus C-14.
3. Average atomic mass means that all of the isotopes of an element are added together (both protons and neutrons), and then averaged.
E. Each group contained a different number of pennies made before 1982 and after 1982.
F. Answers will vary.

Carbon Dating: Reinforcement Activity (p. 33)

1. Carbon dating uses the decay rate of C-14 to tell us when something died.
2. They have different numbers of neutrons. C-12 has 6 neutrons, while C-13 has 7, and C-14 has 8.
3. C-14 is made in the upper atmosphere.
4. Plants use CO_2 for photosynthesis, and animals eat plants.
5. The amount of C-14 has diminished so much that the dating might be inaccurate.
6. ratio of C-14 to C-12
7. Carbon-12, Carbon-14
8. nuclear testing
9. Nitrogen-14
10. Carbon dating in the 1950s
11. decayed
12. half-life
13. ocean or sea objects
14. 50,000
15. Uranium-235

Radioactive Decay of the Penny: Activity and Investigation (p. 35)

1. half   2. Answers will vary.   3. 4–6
4. Answers will vary.

Atoms Crossword Puzzle (p. 39)

(crossword grid)

Atoms Unit Test (p. 42–43)

Part I.
1. a   2. b   3. d   4. d   5. c
6. b   7. b

Part II.
8. a   9. c   10. c   11. b   12. a
13. b

Part III.
1. g   2. j   3. c   4. h   5. l
6. a   7. d   8. b   9. m   10. f
11. n   12. e   13. k   14. i

Part IV.
Answers will vary. Teacher check.